A Butterfly's Wing

for John, Hannah, Scott and Jessica

What have these lonely mountains worth revealing?
More glory and more grief than I can tell:
The earth that wakes one human heart to feeling
Can centre both the worlds of Heaven and Hell.

– 'Stanzas', Emily Brontë

A Butterfly's Wing

Vivienne McKechnie

ARLEN HOUSE

A Butterfly's Wing

is published in 2014 by
ARLEN HOUSE
42 Grange Abbey Road
Baldoyle
Dublin 13, Ireland
Phone: 00 353 86 8207617
Email: arlenhouse@gmail.com
arlenhouse.blogspot.com

International distribution
SYRACUSE UNIVERSITY PRESS
621 Skytop Road, Suite 110
Syracuse, NY 13244–5290
Phone: 315–443–5534/Facs: 315–443–5545
Email: supress@syr.edu
www.syracuseuniversitypress.syr.edu

978–1–85132–092–9, paperback

Design ¦ Arlen House

Front cover painting:
'Butterfly' by Robert Ryan
2008, oil on canvas over board, 57cm by 65cm
www.robertryanireland.com

Back cover image:
'Butterflies in Flight' by Rebekah Pearson
watercolour, ink and collage
www.rebekahpearson.com

CONTENTS

A Shoot

A theme evades me –
the power of thought brushes past me.
I wait crouched, eager to pounce,
but I miss, am missed, don't meet the mark.
More movement.
I wait, pretending disinterest.
I garden, weeding out the rubbish
of winter, a dull brown soil.

Then there is a shoot –
something stirs, maybe only a memory
but the movement marks the page,
the curl of the word begins
and the feel of spring emerges.

Light's Lift

Light lengthens a little stretching towards spring,
slowly, one minute a day,
a miniscule lift, barely perceptible.

Sadness lifts, moving upwards,
the sun becomes the ray, the beam
the way out.

Light lengthens a little stretching towards spring
but slowly, a minute at a time,
the sky's incandescent transformation
is weighted some days
by black bulbous clouds
hanging heavily above,
higher than in winter
but ominous enough to hold back
spring's yellow surge.

Light lengthens a little stretching towards spring
but slowly, a minute at a time,
a cautious step, a tentative touch,
a moment's radiance,
before hiding again hindered by
winter's reluctant leave-taking.

And suddenly it is Spring.
Days are stretched out fully,
the sun beams down
lifting the lines off faces,
revealing the teeth long lost inside.
Arms and necks appear
released from coats' constraint.

Now night is never all encompassing,
day pushes night to a backdrop
until the dark is only a shadow
and the weight of winter lightens
and light's length holds.

In the Stillness of Night

I lie in the stillness of the night,
listen then to the only sound which lingers:
the cuckoo clock announcing over and over
morning's approach.
I lie listening in the dark of this room.
You are beside me, unreachable
across the divide of duvet,
snuggled or burrowed into your side,
you sail on your solitary ship,
your journey only sometimes punctuated by snores.
Once you call out and I cannot hear the name.
I cannot follow even in my imagination.
I am awake and I lie still, trying to sink down,
down into sleep's cradle to join your journey.
The moon is hidden by a starless dark.
I listen to the rain against the skylight,
to the rattle of the window which needs mending.
As the cuckoo announces another hour
I hear a dog bark and a fox
somewhere in the deep, black night
shouts a reply, secure in his freedom,
intent on his search.
Then suddenly the moon appears
pushing aside the murkiness, the pitchy darkness.
The white face teasing the sleeper
pretending it is now day.
You wake for a moment, but are reassured,
the luminous clock does not lie,
the numbers tell more quickly than the cuckoo
it is still night. Morning is hours away.
You drift off again, back to the world without
boundaries,
venturing to the bizarre uncharted ocean

where a wave washing over one leaves only sand in its
wake.
I long to follow, lie waiting
as eager as the traveller at the ship's wharf.
But I cannot go, and you sail away,
too far to reach as morning comes.

Turning Towards Winter

Now as autumn advances
and the wind's edge is sharpened by evening,
the swallow swoops low
weaving a long goodbye.
The light lingers a moment
with spectacle and display
preparing the final show
of orange light on leaves.
The shepherds' delight
in the red sight of evening.
Clouds dash about white and grey
moving hurriedly, busy
as stagehands before the big show.
Winter waits, poised, ready to impress.
The air is filled with colour and movement
as autumn makes a dramatic departure.

Now days contract, closing like penknives
as light shortens towards winter.
The slow minute-by-minute
hurried suddenly by the clock's turn.
An hour gained or lost. Gone
as cold creeps in catching us unawares
chilling insidiously.
And frost follows furtively,
finishing off the plant left
too long outside.
Now winter has arrived.

A Butterfly's Wing

for Mum

Now I linger, looking longingly at every winged being,
knowing the impossibility of a hug,
knowing the fragility of love,
knowing the swiftness of life's flight.

Now, never thinking of you in the earth,
I see you everywhere.
You, who did not lie down willingly,
but who life took in a sudden stroke,
I, who could only stroke your hand and watch
appalled as you slipped the noose of life
and left me numb.
You were silent and elusive, transient
as the butterfly which appeared at your funeral.
It rose delicately out of the lilies which adorned your
coffin
allowing me the poise and sustenance of sudden beauty
to read for your departure.

Now I linger, looking longingly at the Painted Lady
which touches the petals of the rose
and realize that in the fragility of a butterfly's wing
there is strength enough to fly.

Mountaineer

for Iztok Osojnik

The man on the balcony looking down
feels fear.
The man-made sides too sheer, the rail too frail
to hold.
The engineer's design too new, too insecure.
He shudders, leans back, looks up.

The mountain's massive presence fills his eyes.
He remembers
the iron crampon's steel glint, its grip and snag.
He hears
the rope's catch, its taut stretch, the wind's pull and push.
He touches
the pure air in the sway and sag, swing, release and hold.

He feels
the craggy rock's secure, solid surface.
He holds
the mountain's rugged mass a moment, snug there.
He moves
upward, finding firm footholds.
He reaches
the top, rush of wind and the sky's touch.
He breathes
cradled-in cloud, the balcony's shudder a world away.

The woman on the balcony looking up
feels fear.
The mountain's massive, sheer sides loom.
She holds
the solid rail tight to feel secure.
She shudders, leans back and looks down.
The square sides hold the woman safe.

She watches,
waiting, while her coffee chills.
She listens
in the whitening, snow-filled confetti air.
She trembles,
strains forward, searching the distance.

She remembers
their song. Laughter. Chianti lips.
She feels
his caress, her arch up and the full moon and the stars.
She recalls
his face set, quick turn as he moves to his packed bag.
He yields
to the mountain's magnificent, magnetic pull.

The mountain remains unmoved, unchanged.
Man's mastery a miniscule moment
a flash
on rocky sides leading up to the sky.
High above
where clouds hide and reveal its white-topped tips.
A giant Jack and the Beanstalk mystery
to climb.

The stars glisten filling the night's black sky.
She remains
on the solid balcony in darkness.
She hangs
on the firm rail, iron warm in her hand.
She waits.
Silent snow softens the night in flaky down.

The balcony bears the weight of winter days.
The snow still falls in moon-filled albescent nights.
The black ink mountain remains unmoved.

The Magic House of Life

In the magic house of life, butterflies lift,
flitting delicately, silently filling the air,
soundlessly decorating the tropical trees.
Blue and brown, plain and ornate they live
in unhurried splendour for only a short time.
Yet in that short time, in that miniscule life,
they enrich the air, dazzle the eye.

We watch, you and I, as a butterfly is born,
gently easing its way out of the pupa, one stage to
another,
moving to hang for hours, to let the new-made wings
harden for flight, harden for life.

We watch, you and I, while a Tiger lands on your top
resting, startling brown and orange against the white,
you can't feel its weightlessness yet I notice its every
move,
you, who are moving on, stretching out your wings,
hardening for flight, hardening for life.

Laughing at my attempts to entice a butterfly to land
on me,
you gently lift one from the branch and place it on my
finger.
It's heavier than I thought, this world's weight.
This mother's task, this weight, all weight landing on
my hand.
I hold it for just a moment before it flies effortlessly
away.

Suddenly the world outside brightens
and we watch, you and I,
as all the butterflies fill the air above the trees.

We watch mesmerized by the Blue Morpho
the lavish exoticism of the Malay Lacewing. We watch
the King Page spread his wings above the Common Rose
we see that in the bright air the Cloudless Sulphur
is as majestic as the Monarch and as fragile
as the White Tree Nymph fluttering
and dancing in the sun's beams.
Only the baby is still, poised preparing for flight,
patient. Its pupa now the discarded puppet
whose gold warded off the poisonous predators.

We stand a long time while the wings beat soundlessly,
a silent show, and we watch quiescent.
It is only as we turn to leave we see the dying Postman,
its whole being slowly closing down.

Later you and I say goodbye,
each turning, neither looking back.

The Butterflies Dance

Butterflies dance the day in and out, dazzling the eye.
Polkas, gavottes, pirouettes dizzily turning the sky,
making it multi-layered, colouring it orange-spangled.

Butterflies dance the light-filled dance of lanterns
  swaying,
of realms unexplored, of foreign shores and wings.
Alabaster, orange, translucent blue and black, they
  shimmer
against the sky's painted back as they perform their
  delicate show.
Twisting, twirling, spiraling, folding their costumes
  like fans,
changing and hiding, revealing in flirtatious delight.

The Red Admiral's dalliance with the Painted Lady,
his wings fluttering an orange hue, mesmerizing.
A moment's decoration for the sky's pale blue,
with vivid daubs of colour, fragile and transient.
The Dingy Skipper defies his man-made name
with his own dash of brown and amber delight.
The Grayling's rise a lambent sight to catch the eye.
The sun dance of Clouded Yellow and Common Blue
and the purple Pearl Bordered Fritillary, all appear
in nature's play, frivolous, trifling and as swift
as summer lightning or an April shower,
yet as luminous.
Then the Tortoiseshell turns above the nettle,
too quick to be stung and the small Heath's invitation
is ignored by the two Speckled Woods
fluttering and bowing,
winging their own courtship dance.
Butterfly dances to enchant the eye,
to tantalise the heart,

dances as swift as the Purple Hairstreak's dip for
honeydew
in the ancient oak tree's sheltered empire
yet as malingering and as mellifluous.

The butterfly's beauty is at eye level,
no matter how small.
Fanciful, fragile and flimsy they flit from flower to flower
kissing the petals, each movement a tender caress,
a butterfly kiss the lightest of all, the most gentle game,
a touch of eyelashes on cheek but enough to enthral,
to capture even the smallest child, capture us all.

Each sight a symbol of sun and summer, of nature's
radiance.
Yet each wing easy to crush, as ephemeral and as
easily dust.
And each flight a triumph; life's transience masked in
delight.

April

for Dad

I have finished the book you were reading.
I have it here with me still, beside my bed.
A link –
I read on, my thumb, so like your thumb,
was steady, no shaking blurred the words
as I turned the pages to the still end.

You always gripped a book, not held it.
Your hand pressed the page bending it back.
Then later you gripped so hard it hurt.
Terror of falling – the slow pained walk.

But I read the words slowly,
creeping to the end, gently turning each page.
No pressure.
The pressure within, your task incomplete.

What drove me to thumb through this book?
It lay on your bedside table, face down,
its spine cracking, its pages bent.
You lay suspended between the beginning and the end.

Perhaps because in the heat of that day
in the sweat of that afternoon,
in the rarity of that April swelter,
I saw you move too swiftly to a close – burnt out.
Your life lived giving, now given.
And I remained, powerless to call you back,
unable to relight that ember.
So I finished the book you were reading,
and I loved it.

THE PUNGENT SMELL OF A PIPE

Memories flood, filling the already full,
crammed, cobwebby, cramped
room that is my mind.
The pungent smell of a pipe
and you're here:
a gentle medicinal man,
a hand to hold on to,
a welcome relief.
A careful explanation,
a night's sleep   no wrath left.

Now unsteady you reel backwards
and I reel forwards,
no hand to hold on to,
an empty prescription,
the chemist closed,
no relief,
no phone line long enough,
the stretch too taut,
the gap too wide.

And now no prescription can heal.
Nothing can fill the void
now that your final reel
is over.

Ways of Walking

Everyday I walk the bog, two fields away.
Everyday my feet retread some steps of yesterday
and everyday the bog throws up a new display:
the snipe's sudden startling flight,
the pheasant's blustering burst of protest,
the heron's harsh cry, the cuckoo's steady call.
The hare's motionless stance or darting dashes.
The rain soft and gentle caressing my cheek,
or the wind's whipping smack.
Or the breeze rustling the wave of green
or yellow or brown earth my feet tread through.

Everyday I walk the park a drive away.
Everyday my feet repound some path of yesterday
and everyday the park presents a new display:
the magnificent Magnolia and the Weeping Beech,
the unleashed dog's eager escape.
The border's bold lines where no weeds wander.
The keeper's hands turning the soil for the season's
plant.
Here even the crows march majestically and carefully,
cleaning the grass of worms, removing the lunchtime
debris.
The rain soft and gentle, caresses my umbrella.
Or the wind whips, clearing the paths,
leaving the park to wild walkers like me.

Today

They're fishing the river in Limerick today,
bright green-waded men against the sway
and the push and pull of the water's weight,
the tide's swirl and the foam's frothy spray.
There's the swish of the line's cast, the swoop –
mad delight in the line's expectant alight,
and the silent cry as the sound gets caught
in the wind's whirl and the seagull's flight.
Clouds bustle, bunch and swiftly separate,
white tissues on a blue expanse of sky.
They flutter and turn, commanded by
the wind's wild motion and the river's roll.
And the green-clothed men continue to bait
until the reel and a silver splash sends them home.

A Single Shot

in memory of Jerry McCabe

A single shot, or ten?
Does it matter?
We have the scream,
the silence, the end.
Now black plastic
where once was skin.
Concealed you shout out,
standing in horror,
gasping to exclaim
what is it for?
What grieving can erase
the enormity of that sound?
The silence of the end?
The echo of the hunt?
The stillness of broken glass?
Now sirens, the hunt is on.
Road blocks and the chase.
Then the calm of a car, the gentle morning,
the chat shattered by a rage, a need to destroy.
Now no ordinary morning is the same.
We go on, you are still.
Yet still with us, haunting
our apathy, our disregard,
searching out our complacency,
our greedy needs,
our paper demands,
our silent acquiescence.
We can sign our names,
attend the service.
discuss the issue,
argue the point,
exclaim at the awfulness of it all.
And forget by tomorrow.

AGAIN

Once again I am transfixed,
impaled by sights beyond despair.
Midnight's pain: the sweeping aside
of dignity, nature, delight.
Old times gone with a demolition sign.
No retracing or feeling, just flattened lime.
A precedent you'd cry.
Yet what of the old world
worn a long time?
Of the mortar and pain
of ages gone by?
What precedent lets modern minds
exterminate the past's antecedent?
The materialistic surge of modernity.
And ribbons upon ribbons upon ribbons,
not yellow or green, red or gold,
but grey concrete and tarmac which boldly
pronounce the end of an era – for what?

Now the move is from oaks to ash.
Gone is the trees' proud realm.
And Yew trees cry when felled.

THE FIRST COLD SNAP OF MORNING

In the first cold snap of morning
the sun's heat masked
a chill bites my hands.
The horses whinny in white smoke,
we mount, clouds between us
then laughter as we huddle out the gate
and reach the morning –
suddenly sparkling, there
no half measure: night, day.

Red earth swirls under hoof
the pound of sound on soil.
Then the glint of wild wildlife
and yellow eyes peer from the bush.
A surge and we race –
the leopard wins, crouches, watches.
We move away, no challenge.

Tall trees spindly sway at the forest's edge,
bright eyes, bare feet, black faces, white teeth ...
the weightless sound of a shoeless child.
Kikoys flailing in rich patterns of red, yellow, orange,
  green.
Rainbow wearers, nature's opulent abundance
proclaiming Africa!

Eucalyptus trees still sway
tall and lightly leafy.
The swirl of red earth gently dusts
the view ...

Now an impala battles,
his tense yellow body as we set him free,
his black eyes glinting and the stance

to make you do that? How my friends' eyes all widened
over the tops of their beers, and someone muttered, *Dang*,
and I can only imagine how much I'd looked
like a fool, and how you stared me dead in the eye
and said, *I am not apologizing for that*,
then took another swig? And then how the night just went on?
Can your new girl stomach seafood? Even raw?
Is she one of those people who complains that fish tastes
fishy? Like that's a surprise? Does she believe
in salt lamps and Myers-Briggs online assessments?
Is she symmetric and proportional? Does her hair smell
like Christmas? Are her freckles endearing and her music
taste on point? Does she bother you
with incessant chattering when you're trying to fall asleep?
Will she be Mrs. Hamburger Helper?
Will you have some tomboy peapods with exchangeable
boy-girl names? When you cuddle in bed does she ever
run her fingertips down your arm, gaze up and smile,
then ask you to please be nicer to her? Just sometimes?
If it's not too much trouble? Do you still say no?

Every Time an Ex-Boyfriend Calls You *Irrational*, a Woodchuck Gains Its Wings

Rattled & thrown, I leave my bed with its sheets like cold cuts,
each room dimmed the gray of molted feathers. Oh, I'm so calm
until I'm red-tailed & bedeviled in the weeds. I take the rut
instead of the trail. The pond holds November sky serene as palm
against brow, & my God, you sure know how to hollow a heart
of seeds & sinew. So aloof, so cavalier: life must be so easy
for you. Wind loves you! Whistle-pigs love you! The heron parting
from solitary confinement (not so unlike you) loves you! Please
explain this to me: what is it about you? For silence, I stuff
my mouth with milkweed. For stillness, I become a deer
stalking red boughs. I go crazy with your brand of stupid tough.
When I miss you, you write, *I gathered that you want to sever.*
When I raise hell, you say, *Sorry it's been hard*. In the bare trees:
three bluebirds dart the cold. Wait a bit longer for me.

Erasure | Phenomenon

For years and years all I did was say
the hard things

and say them again. But you don't
know how winter

is quiet and loud here.
Your muted

eyes don't see the way
the shadows of trees

render the white slopes
a zebra and what was

water for animals is now ice
and the harried sound

of geese. I wish I could
tell you *you look*

like the scum of the earth today.
Wild things

once circled a town no one
would let them in

and I had to take a class this year
I didn't have a choice

where they taught me to make
words into trees

clauses into forests where nests
knot branches I drew

birds I drew bluebirds and blackbirds
those were the only

colors I had and they took flight
from the page I made

stories with my hands when
I was a child until

I learned to write them down
and the last time

I walked away from a party
this was recently

where everyone was having fun
I cursed my poor

person sweater and I cursed
my boring tears

and have you ever seen a field
where winter moves

in tongues like it's singing out
it's violent and singing

out it's fragile because I have.
It's a delicate process

to roll snowflakes over the ice

the wind must be strong

enough to move them but not

to move them apart.

Self-Portrait with Brown Recluse

Tonight, I have no one to speak to but you,

leggy scab that vanishes in the daylight hours. Dear toxic
listener, you of six eyes, you the color of a bourbon

slow-poured, where do you hold your sadness?

Is it in your venom, your belly, your eight legs? In the mark
of a fiddle on your back, pleading instrument that makes

no sound? I think of my fed-up high school

math teacher mimicking a tiny bow and strings with his hands
while taunting, *Here's the world's smallest violin, playing "my heart*

bleeds for you." Nobody cared. Fiddleback, I'm glad

that you don't have a spine. One of us shouldn't, anyway.
And just as the black widow cradles vengeance in the red

hourglass of her abdomen, so I hold a deep quiver

inside my mouth that never goes away. My boots are heeled
and these nights I drink only river water as I sidestep the fallen

crabapples glistening dark as organs along the road.

I have slept with revenge for years now. Noxious companion,
I confess I wouldn't know if you sought my skin and bit down.

You're the fellow hiding in my shower, the prick

resting inside my shoe, you whose god nestles in the rotting
bark of a woodpile, you who feeds on firebrats and soft-bellied

insects, who is hunted by wolf spiders and centipedes,

who moves throughout the secret crevices and corners of my home
and trails no hoary spark I can find along baseboards, unused

beds, and piled clothes. Our hearts are nothing

but liars and lilac bruises. Old friend, we both want
each other dead tonight. I, too, am learning

to recognize sadness from poison in the dark.

Bastille Day

There are many unplanned ways to say
goodbye: stealing away, making a show,
lying drunk and intertwined in lawns. Against
the washing machine in our friends' sunroom,
this may be the last time I will feel your hands
rub down my legs, even if just to use up
the last drops of bug spray. You touch me
as though I were piebald with bruises. Rebels,
we were too rancorous to celebrate the Fourth,
too jaded for the rural comforts of white bun
hot dogs and watered beer. No matter, I leave
you in a week's time. It has been a day
of crepes and heavy cream, the evening's marvel
smack against clear and green wine bottles.
The humid air is a dress of cigarette smoke.
We eat escargot and frog legs, each their own
rubber squeal. I do not understand love's
cruel assemblage: how from across the room
your face still brightens to me like the rainbowed
coin of sunlight sweetening up a blank wall.
Why on earth am I still pretending? What good
is free will when all the fiddlers inside my chest
are causing such an uproar? How desperate
am I to leave my mark on you even when this day
already feels as distant as a history lesson,
pressing and surreal as a briny mouthful of stars.

Hideaway

A map tells me I am just shy
of a thousand miles from the sand

pine nodding outside your window.
Each state between us jangles

like a coin box. Each city: an insect-
hole. I am too broke to come visit

you, and even so I have become
as small to you as the leak inside

a cup of water. A clean getaway
is just a row of bridges walled in

by fog's cold mushroom. I imagine,
now, how you gaze at someone new:

her eyes, the bright keys, her auburn
hair, the soft pages of that book

you'll tell her you love. It is time
that I must let this little fish

slip from my hand, even as I am
blinded by all the salt of this world.

Fourteen

and bandy-legged, I passed time
        among hills and hay, swam in dirty
pools. The summer skies were green-

eyed, the color of witches and grassy
        cow pies. I was greedy for blue.
In the fields, in the high school with no AC,

men with big teeth scolded girls' skin.
        Shirts must cover shoulders.
Shorts must be longer than arms can swing.

Our bodies were symmetry or else
        scandal. After the horse
crushed my toenail, I chewed the rim

off a Dixie cup of Kool-Aid
        while a clutch of girls prayed
my foot would heal. I wished

the horse in the field would feel pain.
        Later a boy I didn't know
grabbed my ponytail at a football game

and breathed in my hair in front
        of my father, who described it
to everyone around: *he was intoxicated*

by her, that boy, and I was mortified.
        I had powers yet to be harnessed,
ones I couldn't name. I tell you,

I willed it, and that horse: it went lame.

Thief Hallow Branch, Arkansas

Sometimes a ghost is not a ghost
but a column of light. A man's voice

mists in the cottonwoods, speaks
her name over and over, smooth

as egg and butter pie. A girl can't wear
a skirt above her knees in this town.

Watch the red hens, how they squat
and murmur in their scratching

when they fear roughed hands, how
she can't walk the night bridges alone.

Watch the first forsythia creeping up
the road, petals yellow as a thumb-

pressed bruise. By evening, a faint
smell of smoked ribs. Here, spring

keeps the women cold for so long.
Rain curls its fingers into hooks.

He Takes Her

The story is an old one—
a man wants a girl and so

he takes her. Girls are locked inside houses. Girls crawl

naked from dog leashes,
Duct tape slapped across wet

mouths. *I hacked my hair with garden shears, the limp*

pigtails bright as snakes in the grass.
A man sits in jellied luxury

and watches, his shoulders rounded as beef rump.

There's only so much shame
a body can bleed

out in the yard where even cheap lights can't shine.

Girls do not speak.

If I Start Talking About It Now I Won't Stop Hollering

A man once told me sweetness
was the highest quality a woman

could own then put my name
down as *Trouble* in his phone.

And here I've gone
and said too much already,

for this is the country of fat
threading through muscle,

the land that bleeds corn syrup
and brown rivers that flow

in directions I can never
recall. *Stop speaking. Now smile.*

This is how you keep
a story from being told—

mothers teach daughters
what knowledge they write

in bloodlines and what they must
trace into silt or wet snow,

each letter erasing itself as soon
as it's exposed. I have learned

that sweetness is love
    thrown back in my face.

I have spread a map across
    my knees and dreamt of all

the places I could flee—
    the better states (not many

after all) with better laws
    (my body still not my body

wherever the corn oil sun
    rises and falls) and then I saw

a picture of myself as if
    from afar listening again

to your endless white boy
    search for God—oh, there's

the God in your weekly
    poker game, God in your

grandfather's barn, God
    in your goddamn manifesto

on human consciousness,
    God in your marriage

to a much younger girl
    who believes you've hung

the moon, and there's God
    in your painted bedroom,

God in the bleakest heart
        of your coldest Midwestern

woods—where any woman
        would be a fool to go alone—

the God who has been there
        for you all along, who was

made to look like you,
        who never wanted me.

They tell me, *Trouble,*
        let down your hair. Use it to hide

your eyes. Tell me how,
        then, do I still see shame

as it courses through
        the aching silence of lineage,

this rusted river that stains
        its color on my hands?

The Waiting Girl Sweats Out a Fever

After the rain you return to the house
whose drawers fill with mud and fish

scales. When I talk to women, we walk
through ragged weeds and pinch

wild strawberries from stem. They taste
like air. We boil dumplings, sweaty

as hands. When I talk to men, we drink
whiskey. We drink thundered glass. I want

to throw a bottle against the wall.
I want to punch somebody in the head.

I cannot survive the drought this way—
sucking rocks for water, crushing

pine needles into spice, curling in puddled
shade. Without rain the night is polished

as bone. You are the mosquito stinging
through my poisoned dress. You are cheap

cloth puckered into dimples, and everyone
sees. I sleep wet in the scalp and legs.

I dream that a man dies of thirst in a cave
and his body becomes a cat's. His eyes

are dark as a horse's and round as stones.
I press them down, yet they will not close.

The one drag show in town is closing

and tonight the snow is a performance,
    the way it changes light and sound.

Lit windows poke out, fish eyes
    under the alien sky.

Our hostess sashays across the floor,
    leans over our chairs and hooks

our purse straps with one finger.
    This is the cheap bitches table over here!

she hoots to the crowd. We laugh
    at ourselves. *This shit looks like*

you got it at the airport! Praise be
    her silicon cheekbones, perfect

scoops of cream. Praise be
    her russet wig and feral cat

eyes, her dress made out
    of neon straws. We dance.

Champagne bleeds from plastic
    flutes, pools around the table.

From here we can forget
    our circumference of soy and corn,

blind as we are to the smoke
stacks at the edge of town,

their smog sometimes white,
sometimes gray, sometimes gold.

This is mid-winter in mid-country:
luxuriating in banality,

the iron trees, clouds the color
of gasoline, austere fields leaking

pleasure. How I long to be undressed
by unshaking hands.

I look into your eyes,
and I am denied. My voice

becomes grass seeds caught
in the wind. But I am a good dog.

Halved pills, stress rash, stolen
television: I don't cry. I don't cry,

though the coyote crouches
on my chest and howls. This club

is bankrupt. No one here pays
for sequins flashing at the throat,

and this is the Midwestern way:
a man who has everything

believes he is bad, sits at home
alone and feels good about it.

The rest of us will dance
tonight with our eyes closed.

The rest of us are in pain.

Show-Me State

A bicycle strung up between trees
in the woods beyond the soybean field

held by wire its wheels unblinking eyes
they can see back before each wildflower

was tagged with a wooden stake green
plastic tied in ribbons back before a snake

long dead was nailed to a telephone pole
back when people were like the river

when they turned back to the woods
for what hurt them knew jewelweed a balm

for stinging nettles and bur oaks for bad
hearts that basswood made ropes and shoes

that creeper vine's blue fruit brought down
a fever and the yellow lady slipper called

whippoorwill's shoe eased troubled minds
during restless nights I know the hour

when the night birds sing with morning
someone told me old souls are born in winter

closest to the new year someone told me
very young that red berries could kill us

they are meant for the birds they are meant
for snakes alone in the field the yellow

flowers are brown-eyed the fence birds
are blue I asked the last boy when would you

have said you loved me he said I was waiting
for you I said what would you have done

if I did he said I would not have said it back
I am looking for a scene cut with colors

blue storm over wheat field the black trees
beyond I am waiting for a man who pulls

back the woods where the owls cry out
in day for the way he pulls my hair my mouth

away from his oh doesn't he know I want
everything at once I want to be spinning

in trees I want the wire to break I want
the moment before the moment that I fall—

Home Video, 1987

The apple tree in our backyard truly served no role. We did not gather
the fruit, so they dropped, a carmine heft in dank grass, willed
to summon sweat bees and wasps. I was nearly two, my hair
a white-gold flare, my body not yet trained for how to stand still.
Like an actress in the wings, I waited, hopping on tiptoe,
for my father's voice to ask, *Pick me an apple, Annie*. He was proud
of the fresh knowledge in my mind. I was eager to show
him I could choose from the tree that sprawled over our fence, boughs
laden with maroon bulbs. I plucked one and rushed to him, my face bright
with glee. He murmured, *Doesn't look too good, does it?* and palmed
it like a baseball. Member of the rose family, skin rough and tight,
their color less claret and more brown, the fruit in our yard was flawed.
Still I brought him all the bruised ones, the ones torn with rot and bugs.
No matter. He would've let me take down the whole tree with his love.

Dock and Withers

Nothing's about what it's about anymore—
Trailers populate

the horse pasture. Sheep clump the hillside

and cows wade into low pools.
A hoof is living, an intricate

lantern: coffin bone, cannon bone,
sensitive and insensitive

frogs. A boy slaps a frog in a water jar. I talk to you

in my sleep about Jackson and I remember
the gray horse in Tennessee

that watched me swing until I became too grown
for the swing,

the years blurring a sealed window. There are so many

things you are silent about. Watch me unzip
weeds along the fence line.

What's wild can wait in glass.

Rather than run into you at a bar, I drove out for an hour on gravel roads

to a nonprofit wolf preserve, or so
it had been advertised, but what I found
was the owner's husband—his face purpled,

his eyes dead-black, hands in flight
like hostile crows—outside the visitors'
center while she went back in to run

the gift shop of Sunday school needlepoints
and Icee Pops. The man was a Bible-
thumper, a Vietnam vet who preached at us,

an odd gaggle of tourists and locals,
for an hour in the mid-afternoon July sun,
first about the Revolutionary War,

then about Second Amendment rights
(as everyone but me nodded along)
and then finally about the true moral compass

of the wolf pack, as *the ideal family, the closest*
thing to God, because didn't we know
that *wolves don't cheat on their spouses,*

wolves don't molest, don't steal or join gangs,
wolves don't do drugs, and *Bill Clinton*
could learn a lot from these wolves, and that fellow

John Edwards could, too. There was not much
I could do but pay a twenty to run
my fingers through a tamed Gray's coat

as it passed by, its fur coarse and greasy
and unlike any dog's, even though he said
it would be *just like your dog's at home*.

But when the man told us to howl, shapes
I had not seen before began to shift
among the trees without meaning to—a trick

of the light, a flicker of rain—save
for what rose in their blood, after all this time
asleep, for what couldn't be undone.

A Beautiful Night for a Biscuit Truck

Who does well in this town where night flaunts
her ragged satin, her snaggletoothed mouth
of stars and moon? Not the processed steak
encased in dirty ice, nor the crocuses
unfurled amid street clutter. Not the rabbits,
those gray disciples haloed in headlights,
nor the terrified buck that hurled itself
through parking lots, its legacy a bloody
hoof print stamped into a truck's hood.
I never hear trains anymore. In the square,
the dancer's statue dulls from lack
of eyes. Another night drags on, the biscuit
truck's beam a satellite among the bars
that spit out drunk college kids who scatter
like minnows. In this town where hands
are too polite to roam, I remember the place
where night slashed herself on palm fronds
and swayed in a heat that knows the open lips
of a loaded gun, where the guilt I devoured
dripped with honey, and I clung on to whatever
man I loved, as if at any moment my life
could be wrenched from my hands and had.

The month after the cruelest month

is silk and velvet, redbuds and forsythia,
lace-white pear trees backlit

in a streetlamp's planetary glow.
A grinning dog chases cars in tall grass's

gold tassels, and some fool
burns wet green wood in the near

distance, the rising smoke in the trees
with a bad smell that creates no heat,

no clear purpose. How I no longer feel
out-of-love but simply *not-loving*.

I established this pattern years ago.
For one month I believe

I'm someone's dream girl. I fall
for someone's charm like a migrating bird—

the bright flicker of feathers, the rare
trill threading the dogwoods—then gone.

I'm down on my luck again, pissing off
every man around. I'm no one's

dream; therefore I am everyone's
foe. Call me *jaded*—it fits

me like a dress that's so tight
I can't properly sit down. Every woman

must come to a crossroads. Oh, charmer,
I have learned your bright alphabet

of night-blooming flowers.
There will always be dirt in your nails

and smoke on your breath.
There will always be smoke in the trees.

Incident in Northwestern Missouri

—For Daisy Coleman, who, at age 14, was drugged, raped,
and left for dead in freezing temperatures in Maryville, Missouri,
the night of January 8, 2012, and survived.

Who's to say I haven't thrown back
what storm was left in me and tried not to visit God,

but the night they burned down
your house, Daisy, I wasn't thinking

about prayer. You could be anywhere
(*very red and very bruised*) almost any girl

(*no socks no coat no shoes*) whose family
dogs were trained to bark for a child

of a rabbit, a child of a deer, and you—
left for dead, bloodletting the snow in your front lawn

(*frostbite on hands and feet,*
icy chunks in hair). Daisy, more and more

I wake to something sharp
as gunshots, to the garbled plastic sounds

of what happens after words choke
and dissolve and I'm the only one who hears.

The night you tried to kill yourself
for the second time you saw ghosts but no one

believed you, did they?
A girl scarcely lives before she's a lie.

In my new house, I scatter cinnamon
like a séance and rub down the cabinets with vinegar.

I claim it's to rid the ants but ritual,
Daisy, is what keeps us going and I don't need

to tell you what it looks like underneath a scar.
It's a lake, a forest, or worse—because we could

be anywhere but we're here
in Missouri where fences don't appear electric

yet warn against hands, houses smolder
from matches lit by politicians' sons and football kings

and where a godforsaken heart
is a self-fulfilled prophecy for those

who've forgotten how to pray, and Daisy,
could we blame them? You know how forgiveness

is crumbled starlight in the trees
and salvation (*she is nothing!*) rises ugly as healing skin.

Hypochondria

My body needs something to be wrong.   You

filled me

like a cup   and then you

left. I scrub mouse blood

from the baseboards. I scrape frozen bird shit

from the front door.

The smell of death lifts

up the walls.   Still small animals want in.

An orange cat tosses a rag of a rabbit, whiskers it
with claws.

If you knew how the body can clench

and hold: a quickening

of the guts and lungs.

I once had succulents—the man
who broke

in smashed them from the windowsill, and now I

eat a little less, a little
   less not because I want

to be a light bulb but because I need   to be lantern. Forever

winter, the sky looks cold, pink as a clot   in the mouth.

Survival Tactics

Bless the June rains rolling down the Big Muddy,
the river-choked fields dried out in smear
and clod. Bluebirds baffle barbed wire. A puppy flops
in a vegetable plot. Bless the snake and worm
together, their bodies a crooked lecture. Before you met me,
I made my heart a basket of empty laundry. I drank
something pink and feral, watched as I drove away
and everyone stood behind in the gravel. How easy now
the trees perform an alien ballet, front-lit to neon.
Some families play music, see ghosts. I do not know
where my family comes from or why maps pucker up
for this place where the cottonwoods cast out their seeds
to strike water in such brazen display—oh, bless them.

White and Rain

Sometimes a ghost is not a ghost
but a trail of white footprints

down a hall. From Ohio to Florida
valleys flood with mud and salt,

the magnolia flowers dirty as wet
newspapers, too heavy for arms.

Brides dip backwards, feet perfect
as snails. They cut damp cakes

into squares. West of Mississippi,
heat lightning sizzles the dry grass.

Drought makes us lighter, and I
can see through everything now:

sparrow bones, possum bones,
bones of the heart wound tight

as a clock, its key a rain-shaped
word I don't yet understand.

After Yet Another Man Tells Me *I Don't Want to Hurt You*

Because after we slaughtered the lamb, I stayed
and helped to skin the head and cut out the tongue.
Because my tongue weighs heavy as a key, and I, too, can be
just as brass. Because I sleep near a steak knife

where condoms should go. Because I'm only missing
a rib, which I like to think a bird of prey flew off
with in its talons—a curved arrow, a piece of moon, a fang.
Call me *salted away* and not *withheld*. Call me a rabbit

and not a speeding car. And you're the gallant one,
aren't you? So noble, always doing the right thing. Why,
you're a regular squire! Never lily-livered. Never false-
hearted. Because it's not like every woman wasn't already

stunned from the moment a man rolled off her
and called her a mistake, from the moment she was forced
to lie there like an old farm tool because what else
could she do, really, and then later she walked

down the street to her job and another man barked
at her, *Smile!* Because wouldn't she look so much prettier?
Because no wonder he left—and how kind of him
not to lead her on, how valiant to know his own heart

right from the get-go. Because you're a constellation
that light pollution has faded over time. Call me
a table built from barn wood. Call me a bucket of ashes
and rain set out by the front door. And call me tender-

hearted, if you must, because when I sliced off
the dead lamb's ear, I did so lovingly, which means
without flinching. Because it was one of the only parts
we didn't freeze for winter, didn't right then and there

boil or fry up or stew. Because some things are meant to be
discarded, and because you just can't help the way you feel,
like how I cut the skin from the bone and it yielded
to my knife, but I wouldn't call it soft.

Disassociation

Oh, every season is long for you now
especially in Missouri, where you're bound

to be restless in the honeysuckle
light of June evenings. But things happen

every day without your knowing:
your oven ticks as it warms, a slug

drowns in your bathtub, the chopper
flies so low your windowpanes rattle

(whom was it looking for?), your lover
and your friend text each other,

I hate you. You've had a rough go.
It's hard to regain one's reputation

after throwing a wig into a dancing
crowd, but no one can tell you, *Be more*

approachable, when you must dip
your nails into your beer to test

for roofies (there's a polish for that now)
and all the windows in your house

are cricketed with alarms. Look at you
here in your thin cotton dress, pulling

at the threads that shorten your hem.
Look at the scuffmarks on your new

white boots. You refuse to ever be
the girl next door. Still you blame

the cracks in the walls for the poison
you spray every morning then wait

with the door open for it to dry. It's true
what they say: the men who've known

you before see you differently now.
A man asks, *What's your name?* and you're

the one to respond, *It doesn't matter.*
They don't want to remember

and you'll admit it: I've occupied
the darkest times in their lives.

Sapwood, Heartwood, Pith

I went on my own for a while. You couldn't

find me and you didn't dare try. On my way

to school one day I stopped and watched

two workers cut a large oak into six-foot logs.

A rope hoisted one man around his waist;

the other directed from below. I stood

close enough to smell their chewing tobacco

and the sawdust that flaked the heap of branches

with leaves green as bottle shards. I held my breath

as each log thudded to the ground, their hits

colossal and earth-strong. Each time, I clenched

my fists and jaw. That whole day I felt sad

for useless things and how you taught me to see

my own body—parceled, some parts

that you desired, some parts that you jeered,

and how I couldn't un-see myself that way,

even after years. But then the next day I walked

the same path and there it was, ancient disease

darkly worming the stump's rough-hewn maw.

I tell you, after you left me with something

like sickness, something like shame,

I waited for so long to feel whole again

while you went on not worrying, not thinking,

really, at all, and I'm not supposed

to write about what happened.

In my house where I live alone,

I touch my foot to the floorboard

where the wood has rotted away.

I say: here is where I will try

and here is where I will try again.

You apologized to me in the passive voice

and when I pointed it out, you scrubbed me
from your story. I'm not perfect, but at least I try
to always make my voice direct: subject, verb,

object. One of the earliest lessons
in language, owning your shit. Even animals
know that. Sheep can't eat copper

but they will. Chickens can't eat apple cores,
potatoes, or tomatoes. A flash of blood winks
in the yolk, grows cold, and won't ever

become an embryo. Move on. Donkeys protect
the herd, will kill a coyote or a dog. Deer lie
down like dogs (have you ever noticed?)

and a donkey brays like a porch swing swung
too hard. When we were together, you did
things to me but never really saw me.

So you did things to yourself, your past
and your future, to another girl with brighter hair,
another girl who wasn't there. Sheep can read

faces better than you. They know when it's time
to feed or slaughter. A lamb bucked and ran
up the hillside, a pail's metal handle looped

around its neck. I tried to chase it back down
but there was no give, no take. And I've read
that green eyes are the rarest, but people who look

at me directly are pretty rare, too. If you scare
away the herd, the lone sheep or goat will follow.
If you truly want to become a better person,

you should at least drink a different beer
than the one you had before. I'm so sick of you,
I don't even like you, and we had to off

the rooster because it hurt three hens so bad,
their feathers torn out from their backsides,
pimpled skin glowing through. And now they have

to walk around opened up like that while the rest
of the flock stays whole. I remember how
you said to me, *I'm sorry you got hurt. I'm sorry,*

but the damage is done. The damage is always done.
I try my best to ignore you, but here you are
again, coming back to do me in. Old like nature.

Old like a country song. My heart's only a skin
that's bitten through, a young peach I mistook
for a nectarine. Sometimes animals sound

like they are speaking or rather mocking
the way people make animal sounds. Let's see
how you like it: we'll go on and have it your way.

You're active, and I'm passive. I tried
to call you, but my phone was filled with water.
I tried to talk to you, but I was choked.

He Hates What I Do

I am insufferably cruel.
I stand in the yard, bruise-legged

with wet shoes.

The rough man at the bar—
he hates what I do.

Smell the sick human of his skin.
Taste the sour winter whiskering his breath.

He lectures me and I see tin, gray fur,
a splotch of beans on the floor. *I am better*

than McCarthy and Faulkner. No one is greater
than Nabokov. He curses. *Poetry is shit compared to prose.*

I laugh the laugh that hurts the next day.
I laugh the laugh of a cocktease, not a whore.

*

I hollowed out for a man when I was twenty-four.

*

The one I loved mocked my hipbones
jutting up like knives. He'd had

a married woman once (*a very poor girl*)
then his boss, two students (*they were sort-of former*).

He'd won a steak dinner

(a gentleman's agreement)

for which housemate would be first to fuck
their landlord's brown-skinned daughter,

he bragged to me as he threw a dart
against a door. How I hate the chiseled meat

with its tar gristle and lines of fat gleaming
like worms. I don't want to forget

the deer carcass I found decaying
in a creek bed, her ribcage tacky with blood.

*

I had to hollow out to echo.
I had to squeeze my heart to become strong.

*

You're wasting your talents on poetry, the rough man
slurs to me at the bar. He's wanted me

for three years now. I feel his hands
root around in my dress. He's lost something

inside me. He doesn't get
what he doesn't wait for. How forlorn

it is to stare into night's bald eye and be alone.
He hates the selfish thing that I do.

*

Hens peck seeds from my outstretched hand.
My legs are painted black and yellow—

my shins took the brunt

when I went down. I'm the lucky one. Stairs
have no words. I was not pushed. I fell.

The hens eat with a light touch, soft pinches
that do not hurt me after all.

Little Birds

What is it about the December woods
that makes me lonesome? The sky glows

a pale maple syrup, parceled in stained
glass between branches. My breath snags

on cold as I run through. Every house I pass
slumbers peaceful as a cat, every lamp

murmuring *fine, fine*. Frozen creeks
lumber under bridges, the long back

of some forsaken creature who'd rather not
weigh in. It's hard to be both large and shy.

And my heart is a spilled
glass of wine—blot it with paper towels,

throw salt on it, sponge it with shampoo, dab it
with white vinegar. I cannot reason the silver

linings—aluminum foil scrunched
around saplings' roots to keep away

slugs and sunscald—the snap of a book closing, the aloof
space in bed, the words I dread that come

after a chair's resolved groan:
I need to talk to you. I turn at a fluorescent light

stamped into a wooden post. Truly, I cannot fathom
the dodged bullets that dotted deer hides

instead of mine. Finches charm dead
leaves, rucked as gloveless hands. Tonight, let me

gather everything dead or dying in my arms. The sky
is blank as a pie plate, yet it will not snow.

The Waiting Girl Feels a Pulsing Where There Is No Child

When they say I am nothing like my family,
everywhere I begin to see my son.
The days loll into clammy pages, stain

my hands indigo. This is what cleaning
affords me: a soup lid in a trash bag slices
my leg. Blood smears dirty plastic.

I smash the coffee pot on the counter.
If glass is bound to break, then why
am I surprised when shards glitter

with dust and prick my bare soles?
In the scorched bar yard a long-legged
rabbit darts between pizza crusts

and cigarette butts. The sky churns
pewter and olive, drips muddy into day-
drinks. Little bunny, this fairy tale

is an ugly one. There won't be bonnets,
no nursery painted cream and blue.
Those that I have loved, they've made

themselves strangers to me now. My child,
wait for me in darkness. These godless
men are not worthy of your name.

Your Name in My Boot

I put your name in my boot. I wrote it
on a piece of paper and ground it with my heel.
Spider-bitten, knee-bruised,

the year began. I looked up and found
the Milky Way, a ghost pinned
to the ceiling, its eyes as sure as stars.

I spilled ink on your fortune
and then you appeared at my door,
a bodiless wind. In what's left of the wild,

there grows a weed called doll's eyes.
A man asked, *Have you been here this whole time?*
I was invisible until I drew on my eyes.

So is it you or me who cannot see clearly?
I picked the weed named Adam and Eve.
Blue-eyed grass, blue-eyed Mary, ghost plant,

woman's tobacco, touch-me-not, false
sunflower also called yellow star—you blooms
are all a tease. I was born for root-food,

corn-planting, hot sun, short harvest, red plum.
A man asked, *Did that all really happen to you?*
I thought you were a good man, but you have

less and less to say. I traced your name
in the river. I drew your name on the wall.
Northern fires stain the pink moon red,

and the year begins its ancient end—
leaf-falling, deer-mating, fur-pelts, wolves
revised to coyotes I only see beside the road.

Sometimes they're dead, but sometimes
they're a flash of copper and gold.
I froze your name into the snow.

My hips ached. My leather split, and my heel
caught a slick wooden stair. Blood
matted my hair, and I don't remember

leaving. Blood moon, hunter's moon,
oak's moon, cold moon, long night's moon—
it's been the longest time here.

A man asked, *Why are you always alone*?
I put your name in my boot as I walk away.
You'll never forget my own.

Still Haunted

A stranger to this winter city flushed blue
        with fallen snow, I touch metal to make light
to walk until I think I break a train. A rough

voice jeers at me, *What the hell is wrong with you?*
        Mathematics informs me I no longer want
you. Still, I remain the one who slinks

down to a wet and wretched creature
        when I see your face: still, my voice
catches in my throat hard as a coin. Still,

my hands shake pallid as a specter even
        after two years without your body near.
On the north side of town, littlenecks

coddle in warm butter while girls in black
        boots tromp through curbside pots of slush
and gasoline. Over wine sparkling in tavern

firelight, my most logical friend tells me
        how she once met a ghost on the stairs
of the old house we shared years ago,

how she first heard the footsteps of nothing
        at all, then felt a gust of cold air as it passed
her by. Her eyes fearful, she did not deserve

this witching hour affliction from a spirit
        she has since learned was a girl scorned
by her family for running off with an artist,

her unseen phantom only women now
          can sense, and in a house of eight women,
only my friend. Why wasn't it lovelorn me?

New city, new lovers, nothing matters. Spirit,
          on a snow-laced street, you are the lamppost
caught wild in flame. This you still know:

if I sensed your footsteps racing towards me,
          if I felt your rush and if I heard you call out
my name, Spirit, still, I would turn.

In Defense of Not Getting Over It, at Least Not for Now

An artist friend told me that her favorite subjects to draw
were those she could not depict all at once: the drunken geometry
of an old house, a majestic pine, our town's river in its lawful
currents—the sky reflected in water the dull-bright colors of money,
but pure. She came back every day to a new vantage point, a new angle,
and that became her blessing and her curse, the way she must return.
Summer, I washed dishes to pay a fee. There was one pot I'd wrangle
with for hours—the bane of my evenings, a Herculean feat earned
by its height that reached my knees; its girth, my embrace could not hold.
Someone always burned sauce at the bottom, a thick char that gleamed
despite a soak with dish soap, a dusting of baking soda, a controlled
boil on the stove. There's beauty in it, though: the slow work of dreams
unreached, revision's stench and steam. It's all meant to train one's heart.
I have learned how to build something first by how to take it apart.

Salt Creek, Missouri

Sometimes a ghost is not a ghost
but a woman who hates me a thousand

miles eastward. There is nothing
I can do here but palm the weight

of hailstones, wear the green rain
as a veil. Two hens named for country

stars attack a hen named for a queen.
There is no one I can ever be

to her than the brat her husband loved
first. Trees wring bare hands: winter.

Dog-tooth violets flirt with soft earth:
nearly. I once had a plan to forget him.

How futile our backstory, how
precious her grudge. Today, I drive out

to the field with five white horses
just to make sure they haven't been sold.

Midwestern Litany

Wouldn't give my heart to the railroad.

Wouldn't give my heart to an old dog.

Not for rusted lace or seed pearls.

Not for bone china or barely dented silver.

Not even this old house, the walls flaking off like hardened sugar.

Wouldn't give my heart to hog corn.

Not for the promise of dyed flowers.

Wouldn't give it to the bridge over the river.

And no, not for penicillin.

Not for coffee hot in Styrofoam or the smell of burning leaves.

Not for dark meat.

Not for pelicans in a soybean field stubbled by winter

that follow the river currents north, then south once more.

Not for baked apples in nutmeg and butter.

Not in this land exhausted of color.

Not for beer the color of dirt, for dirt the color of blood.

Wouldn't give my heart to the ghosts of deer

or for violence in Illinois—I saw that doe throw her body

in front of an eighteen-wheeler—she died in a pinwheel

explosion—she was alive and leaping

and then she wasn't—she didn't even look.

And it's not easy to hide in a flattened land

with hearts beating and stopping on every billboard.

Wouldn't give my heart for the threat of hell.

Not for dead leaves curled like fists on the vine.

Not for my body within my body.

Not for rain that turns the fields to ice, my car to ice, the trees—

the highway

that would carry me to the mountains,

to the swamps, the canyons, the sea—if I let it.

Wouldn't give my heart to the telephone wires.

Wouldn't even give my heart to the sun

melting the whitened fields and revealing what is blue,

so why would you think

why would you think

why would you think (I didn't even look)

that I would give my heart to you?

Site Fidelity

I never heard them until I did.
            Coyotes slunk out

            from cornfields and creek beds

their haunches a gold-brown
            rumor in tall grass. The pup

            I found was an offering

for cluster flies, scarcely breathing
            in catalpa's shade.

            A starved creature

begins to resemble its prey: long
            rabbit ears, crooked

            fawn legs. These days

my eyes are painted in shadows.
            I have stared into the black

            river. I have slept

beneath the old moon and woken
            to the ghost of a man

            who turns from me,

fading back into earth's hard soil.
These days I walk

around with a secret

deeper than skin: a bitten cheek,
a burnt tongue.

By autumn's pale sun,

the coyotes return to the fields.
Through the day

through the night

I can still hear their mournful
howls. Believe me:

I tried to save a life.

I carried a pan of water.
I shooed away the flies.

Play the Fool

The road was red again. I trespassed
and a horse with a rope halter

but no saddle followed me down
the driveway as would a dog.

I picked up my gait, started to run.
I didn't want it to get too close,

didn't want to lead it to the road.
Once somebody called me

a *shit-magnet*, though lovingly,
and I couldn't disagree. I am prone

to self-injury, predisposed
to locate the most trifling man

in any room. Even when I try
not to host a party I host the party.

And three years later I think
I have finally figured out why

you didn't want me in the way
I wanted you. You asked me

if I needed to hear the reason
and I responded, *Don't tell me,*

because I knew one day I would
find it in a place I shouldn't be.

While foraging for blackberries
in the Tennessee woods, I came

across an abandoned shed rusted
olive, its walls stabbed through

with old tools, and on its deck
out front stood two goats

expectedly as if they were my
neighbors and I had stopped

by to borrow an axe or some eggs.
Animals have no reason to be kind

and really, neither did you. Ducks
will drown a chicken in its own pen.

A ewe will head-butt her own lamb
to feed. Don't mistake obedience

for a gentle heart. I understand
now what you wanted. The horse

reached the fence post by the road.
I hid behind the tulip poplar

and when it couldn't see me any
longer, it swung around as though

in two parts: first the gray neck,
then the dappled torso, and turned

back up the driveway to its home,
despondently, but with purpose.

The Encounter

Late in the day, late into spring, the sky a lilac gauze
over the last flowering trees—their petals curled
as if singed, the new green pushing beyond—
I turned on the path and, for a moment, could not discern
what I'd just come upon: three surprised faces, a trio
of baby possums latched to their mother's back, her head
down, drinking from a rain puddle, then at once keen
and lifted, teeth bared, emitting a low snarl. Wide-eyed,
their ears like button mushrooms, they were nearly
too big to all fit, the third one trailing, barely hanging
on. Frogs sang from their pond. I was not fearful,
though she growled at me as I passed by, brazen
creature who refused to shrink back into the thrum
of new evening, into the wild from where she'd come.

Vow

I will mistake the plop of dew on canvas
for raindrops for footfall. It will be dawn
before dawn. The sky will be no color. The birds'
wings will be pinned in trees, their warbles
unplanned, bright flares, not yet song. I will wake
with a start. I will walk to the river, its water
like watered milk, the mist thick as a layering
of hands, the fishermen in prayer. I will wait there.
It will be a bouquet of dried violets, ornaments
carved from green soap, the blueberry bush
in my childhood backyard, its wire gown glinting
in the sun and the deer gazing on, the berries
before they are berries, pink as rosebuds,
the shells buried beneath sand in hurricanes
that have turned over the sea for centuries,
for a thousand years, the grains of sand colors
beyond colors, their beauty hard-won.
It will be written in salt lines. It will be as old
as every omen, as the music of dying stars,
the soft wings unfurling from a common bird
in the known purpose of her song. I have worlds
of things to tell you. I will give you my word.

Acknowledgments

Many thanks to the editors of the journals where these poems first appeared, some in slightly different versions:

Academy of American Poets: "Midwestern Litany"
The Adroit Journal: "Salt Creek, Missouri," "The month after the cruelest month"
Blackbird: "The one drag show in town is closing"
Catch Up: "If That Isn't a Sign Then God Knows What Is"
The Columbia Review: "Little Birds"
Connotation Press: An Online Artifact: "Science of Uncertainty," "The Waiting Girl Sobers Up in the Same Room as Before"
Copper Nickel: "In Defense of Not Getting Over It, At Least Not for Now"
Crazyhorse: "If I Start Talking About It Now I Won't Stop Hollering," "Prudesville, USA"
DIAGRAM: "Thief Hallow Branch, Arkansas"
Ecotone: "After Yet Another Man Tells Me *I Don't Want to Hurt You*"
Fugue: "Vow"
Grist: "Egg and Ash," "White and Rain"
Gulf Coast: "Bastille Day"
Harpur Palate: "Disassociation"
Memorious: "Hypochondria"
Meridian: "Every Time an Ex-Boyfriend Calls You *Irrational*, a Woodchuck Gains its Wings"
Mid-American Review: "Dock and Withers," "Site Fidelity," "Survival Tactics"
Midway Journal: "Hideaway," "The Waiting Girl Feels a Pulsing Where There Is No Child"
Nashville Review: "A Beautiful Night for a Biscuit Truck"
North American Review: "Hallucinate the House, Hallucinate the Woods"
Paper Darts: "He Vows to Follow Me Even After He Leaves Me"
Phoebe: "Fourteen"
Sonora Review: "Self-Portrait with Brown Recluse"
Third Coast: "Your Name in My Boot"
Thrush Poetry Journal: "The Waiting Girl Sweats Out a Fever"

Tinderbox Poetry Journal: "He Takes Her," "Still Haunted"
Tupelo Quarterly: "The Encounter"
Vox Magazine: "Show-Me State"
Washington Square Review: "Play the Fool," "You apologized to me in the passive voice"

"Incident in Northwest Missouri" first appeared on *Thethe Poetry* as part of the "Political Punch" poetry series and was then reprinted in the anthology *Political Punch: Contemporary Poems on the Politics of Identity*, edited by Erin Elizabeth Smith and Fox Frazier-Foely (Sundress Publications, 2016).

*

I am grateful for the mentorship and wisdom of my doctoral committee, Aliki Barnstone, Cornelius Eady, Alex Socarides, and Mary Jo Neitz, and for the gifts of time and beauty from the residencies at the Vermont Studio Center and the Sundress Academy for the Arts at Firefly Farms, where several of these poems were written.

Thank you to my dear friends and readers Rachel Inez Lane, Brandi Nicole Martin, Greg Allendorf, Heather McGuire, J.D. Smith, Avni Vyas, Candice Wuehle, Amanda Bales, Melissa Range, Austin Segrest, and Vedran Husić, as well as Alyson Thiel, whose art always has eyes and wings. To my Reynolds kin for the brightest fire and friendship. And to my family, Nancy and Scott Barngrover, Kristy and James Clear, and to my grandparents for their unwavering love and support.

To Mary Biddinger, Amy Freels, Jon Miller, and the University of Akron Press: endless gratitude for your exquisite care, your vision, and your steadfast declaration that, no matter what, "Poetry Lives!"

Finally, this book is dedicated to the memories of Monica A. Hand and Naira Kuzmich. As far as being brazen goes, they taught me everything I need to know.

Photo: Heather McGuire

Anne Barngrover is the author of *Yell Hound Blues* (Shipwreckt Books, 2013) and coauthor, with poet Avni Vyas, of the chapbook *Candy in Our Brains* (CutBank, 2014). Her poems have appeared in *Ecotone*, *Crazyhorse*, *Copper Nickel*, *Indiana Review*, and others. Anne earned her MFA from Florida State University and her PhD from University of Missouri. She is an assistant professor of creative writing at Saint Leo University and lives in Tampa, Florida.